Risking Delight

Risking Delight

Poems by

David Stallings

Kelsay Books

© 2018 David Stallings. All rights reserved. This material may not be reproduced in any form, published, reprinted, recorded, performed, broadcast, without the express permission of David Stallings. All such actions are strictly prohibited by law.

Cover Art: Tonti "Leap" tontifineart.com

ISBN: 978-1-947465-76-3

Kelsay Books
Aldrich Press
www.kelsaybooks.com

For the women who taught me the most: Rebecca, Suzanne, Thérèse, Ariel, Andrea; and for Tavi

Acknowledgments

Poems in this collection first appeared in the following publications, at times in different form or under alternate titles:

Bacopa Literary Review: "Ripening" and "Don't get me wrong"
Blue Earth Review: "Nearing 65"
Boston Literary Magazine: "Leaving Nashville, 1952" and "Odonata"
Cascadia Review: "Fool" and "By Resurrection River"
Cirque Journal: "Pose" and "Petition"
Constellations Journal: "At Longs Pass" and "On Holly Farm Lane"
Crab Creek Review: "Loss"
Drawn to Marvel: Poems from the Comic Books: "Off Medial Avenue"
Dunes Review: "He unravels"
Exhibition: "Old Goat Lake"
Existere Journal: "Oracles" and "Back Then"
I-70 Review: "Conception"
KNOCK Magazine: "How It Is Done"
Milk Money: "*Cornus sericia*"
My First Time (anthology): "First Time"
New Millennium Writings: "On North 45th Street"
Out of Our Magazine: "Offense"
Perceptions Literary Magazine: "though never in a Book it lie" and "When you follow the Big Quil's lead"
Picayune Literary Magazine: "Humboldt, Tennessee, 1998"
Platte Valley Review: "Among Her Gifts" and "A Good Day"
Poetry Quarterly: "Trailer"
Riprap Journal: "On a Tuesday"
RiverLit Magazine: "Just This"
Roanoke Review: "On Cold Mountain" and "When We Were Young"
Rock & Sling: "With Us"
Skylark Review: "Prognosis"

Sobotka Literary Magazine: "Sunday Afternoons"
Steam Ticket: "Mudra"
Stoneboat Literary Journal: "Tan Clay" and "No Time"
The Chaffin Journal: "Sorting Things Out"
The Mas Tequila Review: "Leap," "Self-Portrait in Plaster" and "Last Things"
The Raven Chronicles: "From a forested hillside"
The Southern Poetry Anthology, Volume VI, Tennessee: "Message"
Tulip Tree Review: "Endless Knot," "In our beach grass bower" and "Odyssey"
Vagabonds: "Legend" and "Unburdened"

Some of these poems were published in a chapbook, *Resurrection Bay,* Sacramento: Evening Street Press, 2012.

Many thanks to the poetry communities I've studied with, including the Community of Writers at Squaw Valley and Port Townsend Writers' Conference. Special thanks to master poets who have been kind and helpful, including Joe Stroud and Marvin Bell, and to many West Puget Sound poet friends, including longtime workshop leaders John Willson and Nancy Rekow who both provided this collection of poems with a close read.

Special thanks to gifted Northwest artist, Kristen Tonti—my friend and occasional partner in ekphrastic creation. What a pleasure to experience Tonti's art and my poetry interweave, as in her "Leap," shown on the cover of this book, associated with the poem, "Leap," on page 78. For additional information visit tontifineart.com.

I am particularly grateful for Jack Gilbert's lifelong work in poetry. The title of this collection was suggested by his poem, "A Brief for the Defense" (in *Refusing Heaven*, New York: Knopf, 2005).

Contents

I.

Leaving Nashville, 1952

Packed between suitcases, boxes—
back seat of a Buick Dynaflow,

view blocked, air thick with Dick's Camels
and my mother's Herbert Tareytons,

I try to filter my breath
with Kleenex—

but the asthma isn't fooled.
How will I make it all the way to Alaska?

On the way out of town, Dick swings into a gas station.
When the trailer we're towing slows us down

and another car slips in front—
Asshole! my new stepfather roars, and grabs

in the glove box for his .45 automatic.
All I see is his arm

and my mother's grip
on his wrist.

I can barely breathe.

Tan Clay

Soft rain happens upon me
halfway up a high bluff.
The clay slickens, threatens to sluff me

into the Yukon River. Down there
are my mother and stepfather
at an overnight trailer camp

on our migration to Alaska.
My childhood home no longer
exists. My real father is dead.

I slip, catch myself on a root,
close my eyes, breathe deep,
choose a different upward angle.

Again and again I slide,
pause to refill my lungs,
to discover

another way forward. At last,
coated with tan clay, I crawl
over the crumbly ledge, into a cemetery

unlike any I've seen, where wooden burial
boxes, some like little houses, stand weathered
in the rain. I do not know

if I am supposed to be here, but
scooch under a wet roof overhang
to sit and look around

protected
in this tiny
wild home.

Conception

A cloud of wonder and wondering
casts only a slight glow
on the resting couple.

A single candle burns,
only light in the rental apartment
above a rural funeral home

one window ajar to
first warmth of Alabama spring.
Husband and wife whisper,

put aside news of Pacific
defeat, prowling Atlantic U-boats,
his hypertension, her fear

of being alone. As they join,
the cloud melds, absorbs their love,
their fright, curls deep within

her warmth, there to forget
the carnage to come,
his father's imminent

stroke, his mother's years
of loneliness to come.
He, too, will risk delight.

Sunday Afternoons

Two years after the war ended,
when I was five, my daddy
took me along Sunday afternoons
to visit Houck, his childhood friend,
in Nashville's VA hospital.

I had heard the story,
imagined it as my own—

Troop ship
torpedoed
I swim alone
under cold
burning water
clear a hole
come up
for each breath
cannot escape
heat and oil
flooding my lungs
hardly alive
when they pull me out

When we walked the hall
to that hospital room,
I held my daddy's hand tight.

At first in the darkened room
I didn't notice
Houck's waxy disfigurement—
only his tears, his rasping
words of welcome.

Off Medial Avenue

Clad in black, hair combed into
a V on his forehead,
The Avenger slips

from his family's Nashville home
into darkness and power.
With mission *to protect and defend*

he steals through shadow, peers into
Sadie Mack's window, where the widow
sits sewing, listening to the radio.

In silence, he glides
past a row of trimmed shrubs
to the Todds' side yard—eyes just

clearing a family room windowsill as
he spies a third-grade friend, Tony,
snapping his little sister with a red

bath towel. Both are naked.
Their dad yells, *Cut it out!*
Dropping low, The Avenger

scrambles for home. Safe in bed, hair
brushed back, he lies sleepless, smiling—
first taste of the borderlands.

First Time

I had unsuccessful sex,
was whipped for lying and
had an out-of-body experience
all in one afternoon with
Judy Kay, daughter of a Southern Baptist minister
who lived across the street.
When safe aboard the backyard ship we'd
built from boards and cardboard boxes,
I said
          Let's show each other.

Near the fo'c'sle, when I pulled down
my jeans and stretched the top
of my white Jockey briefs,
she craned her neck.
I looked down her belly and saw—
nothing. So where was it?

          What are you doing?
Oh, no— her mother on the back porch.
          Go home and tell your parents
          what you've done!

I ran as never before—
a tempest, a squall, leaping
hedges, fences, a rock wall,
U.S. Keds barely touching ground.

Home, breathing deeply, soaring less,
I became a boy again.
My mother, near the phone, asked,

What happened?

Nothin', I said. *Where's Daddy?*

Gone to cut switches
in case you're not telling
the truth.

Mudra

One night, when he's seven,
he hears his mama say
        Daddy has died, gone forever....
                Remember everything he taught you.

He can only reply
        Daddy showed me just how to dry
        between my legs after a bath.
                I'll remember.

Decades later, little
remains of his father's voice,
his smell, his touch.
Yet every morning

after showering,
he saws a towel forward
and back both sides
of his genitals. It works well,

leaves his crotch
feeling tingly.

Loss

Everything is new:
my mother's cursing husband,
this small Alaska town,
my new
5th grade classmates—
including Larry Sefrovitch
who wants to fight.
A crowd circles us
on the playground
as we flail.
Only after a teacher
pull us apart
do I cry.
I can't stop.

Offense

Hands in jeans, three of us kick at the sidewalk,
wait for the Liberty Theater
to open. My mother has dropped us off

but dammit, is still hanging around
on this sidewalk till the door opens.
Will she never learn?

Ducktail haircuts frozen stiff, we stamp our feet,
beat our arms, huff and puff in this frigid air.
Our clueless scoutmaster walks by, leaps to

conclusion, says *You boys shouldn't be smoking!*
My mother billows a frosty breath, says
Oh, we're all smoking, Mr. Fyle. See?

Later, my friends agree—
You got a pretty
cool mom.

Pose

.410/.22 over-and-under shotgun
across her knee—
my mother scans peaks
above Resurrection River.
Her husband's low camera angle
captures her right foot braced
on a snowbank. She wears
a blue kerchief, red and black
buffalo check jacket—this displaced
Tennessee girl, now 40
with 11-year-old son,
two years into a failing
marriage.
Here she is
still
trying.

How It Is Done

You don't do it that way, sneers
Harvey, our Senior Patrol Leader,
watching us try to tie a bowline.
Scouts must execute everything precisely—
sharpening pocket and hunting knives,
striking flint with steel,
lining up ramrod straight
at troop meetings.
This crazes me and
Harvey's younger brother.

One night in my room,
Harvey guides us in new directions,
molds a clay cock and scrotum,
encourages us to
lower our pants and compare.
Another night he surprises us
with a wooden cock he's carved, asking
How'd you guys think of such a thing?

I soon find a younger boy to groom.

Six merit badges
shy of Eagle,
I quit
the Boy Scouts of America.

By Resurrection River

What happened to this old mutt?
the boy wonders. Late fall
sun doesn't touch

the stretch of potholed road,
the curled paws, this scarred muzzle
of mud-splattered dog

at its edge. The boy
walks on, .22 rifle over his shoulder,
plinking at tin cans

in garbage dumped along
the gravel streambed, till
days later, when the dog lies caked

with debris, belly bloated, the boy
aims, fires a bullet into swollen
gut, staggers back

from the fetid *whoosh*,
watches the belly sink,
imagines a sigh of "thanks."

Next weekend, only fur
tatters along with a few bones.
One week later—nothing.

Petition

He stands alone outside the San Rec Room,
where often he plays ping-pong,
jokes and flirts
with native girls whose parents
live in the TB sanitarium.
He doesn't know why, but this will be
the place, and now will be the time:
Tuesday afternoon, June 26, 1956.
Remember.

Tomorrow they leave.
They've packed up the stick shift '53 Olds
and will *escape from this damned place,*
as his mother and stepfather put it
when not arguing.
He asks, *Why do we have to leave?*
His mother just says,
Alaska hasn't worked out very well.

They'll head for Colorado
where years before they spent
a few days at a stopover
on the way to Alaska.
We were happy there
his mother reminds him.

He's given his collie to the neighbors,
his paper route to his best friend,
said goodbye
to everybody he knows.

Now, right hand on the white wood railing
in front of the rec room door,
he looks up to the clear sky,
reaches out
to his self-to-be:

Please find a way back to this moment.
Please help me understand.
I'm counting on it.

Trailer

He steps off twelve paces to
confirm this rotting hulk,
buried by alder and cedar,
is a 35-footer, like the one
where he lived with his mother
and Dick Cox, his stepfather.

He sets aside bird watching,
tucks binoculars under his shoulder,
steps through pungent decay,
rotting laminates, moldy curtains.
Still, enough remains—
here the tiny bathroom, there the kitchen,
there the foldout dining table.

Up front was a hideaway bed,
all the room he had to himself, where
every morning he folded and put away
sheets and blankets, though he could leave
his army men, his cigar box of treasures,
his books on the windowsill.
Once, at the foot of the bed
he nursed Hey You, his black mutt,
when she'd swallowed a chicken bone.

The far end—*their place*—unknown, forbidden.
Fifty years later he peers into these tatters
of the vanished strangers' bedroom, feels
his mother's and Dick's presence,
hears those nightly cries
of loving and hating
that he could not escape.

Now, a Wilson's warbler sings
from the willows.
Shaking his head
he steps out of shadows,
to focus on this bit of
yellow-feathered life
calling him back
into spring.

II.

Legend

Ariel lolls in lambskin,
burbling December silence
from her mother's back.
After miles of icy forest path,
we inhale the first wafts
of sulfur, cross Boulder Creek,
find a hot pool
over snowy banks.
To avoid tarnish
we remove wedding rings,
embrace our newness
in naked waters.
Through fir and cedar, moonlight
fractals the swirling steam.
Ariel suckles a misty breast,
and for a time
her mother and I melt
our differences within the fiery
tears of those dragons
who fought to a stalemate
above this place
and now grieve alone
in wintry caves.

Just This

A zendo bell concludes
our seven days of silence.
We chatter with others,

clean up the camp,
last to leave,
slow to walk the forest hill.

Near our loaded car,
a late spring trailhead
draws us into woodland,

into songs of western tanager,
Swainson's thrush,
essence of mahonia.

At a trailside
nest—moss and leaf—
we pause and touch,

adorn elderberry with
our clothes, drape our
underwear on fern fronds.

From a nearby rock,
            our empty sandals
                        chant sutras.

Among Her Gifts

Surf roars against Yellow Banks,
this gravelly whoosh of its undertow
chuckled over by western gulls
riding wind and mist.
Her hands butterfly through smoke swirls,
place a silvered driftwood shaving,
a peel of red cedar bark,
a hoard of paper scraps.
She tilts in concentration—
maybe a flat stone windscreen *here*,
to reflect heat
back to the heart.
Into the smudgy warmth she reaches,
senses new life. She kneels,
places cheek to sand,
whispers breath into an ember.

The flame leaps and crackles
promising hot tea and oatmeal,
dry socks, another day.

In our beach grass bower

we roll onto our backs
still entwined
filled with starry brilliance
this light has journeyed
for billions of years
shift one atom
deflect one photon
and none of this
would be

On Holly Farm Lane

Every night I worry
about the ridgepole,
last Doug fir log to be raised atop
this new home we're building—
32 feet end-to-end—
too high up, too unwieldy
to handle as one log.

OK, cut it, I decide.
Butt the two sections
on a bearing wall,
so they'll be strong—
though not strong as one long piece.
Then— oh, shit— what about
the big earthquake?

So, what if I saw
a vertical slot in each butted end,
slide a single steel plate down
into the two slots
then bolt the plate through each log—
sort of like rejoining the two log pieces—
not likely to pull apart,
able to flex a bit at the joint.

Again I visit the stooped old
blacksmith in the Village
who agrees: *A fellow can't be too safe.*
But, you never can tell.
He fashions the perfect plate.

Two days later,
my articulated ridgepole
rests in place
and I'm sleeping better.

Forty years and several quakes later,
this log house still stands strong—
a place to be
when the big one hits—
maybe.

From a forested hillside

our small home has risen,
hand-hewn log by log
notch by notch
until today, with friends,
we lift the Doug fir ridgepole,
set it in place
topped out with a yew branch
nailed to its south end.

Along the way
some accidents—
a little spilled blood,
but plenty of good fortune
like this small, unplanned loft
where you and I will sleep
this night, our first over many years—
where three naked purlins
stretch above us.

Tomorrow
we'll start the roof
but for now
we have this moon, these stars,
this arching madrone—
over our two-year-old daughter
asleep nearby in her bedroom
where you've hung curtains
over an opening,
a window not yet framed.

Don't get me wrong—

for the one that fed me,
I am grateful.
For the one that nourished
my newborn daughter,
I am grateful—
though not enough
to eat it, even when my wife
fries it with onions.
We bury most of it
under the west apple tree.

When my wife becomes
a midwifery teacher,
I support stocking our freezer
with *teaching placentas*—
though when I step barefoot
in the bloody drool
of a thawed organ
left overnight
on the kitchen counter—
then we have to talk.

At first, I find
being encircled
by a sacred ring
of placentas
reassuring.
Thawed, then ritually buried
within the medicine wheel
of our fire-circle meadow,
they honor quietly
the earthy feminine—

although I soon inform my wife
of my need to fell and peel
a stout red cedar,
from which I carve
a 14-foot phallus
to erect in the meadow—
Lord Shiva, surrounded
by placental *dakinis*.

Years later, after our divorce,
after I chainsaw the totem
at ground level,
it still retains
admirable length,
protruding far out the rear
of my Mazda pickup,
red flag flapping,
bound for a different meadow.

Endless Knot

Roll two thin strings of pure gold,
braid each into a sinewy knot—
the Buddha's entrails.
Set each knot in a dark oval at the center
of a white gold band. Both rings
the same, yet different.
We never remove them
except in sulfurous hot springs.

Through years of meditation retreats,
hands in *zazen* mudra,
the pad of my right ring finger
cradles the knotted seal.

After 20 years we grow apart,
bury our rings at the foot
of a favorite old cedar on our land.
One year later, after our divorce,
we each dig our ring from the ground.
Mine rides for years
in the ashtray of my pickup,
bound for Lake of the Angels,
where Ariel was conceived.

Never able to make the toss,
I finally give the ring to Ariel,
who melts old family metal
into amulets.

Even now, while I meditate,
the pad of my right ring finger
finds the strength of that long-absent seal.

At Longs Pass

This trail disappears into nowhere,
gullied out by last fall's downpours,
lost under banks of unmelted snow.

I keep climbing—
6300' pass not far ahead,
trekking poles in rhythm with feet,
detour around an unmovable knot—
four mountain goats—
then ascend two false summits.

A ridge crest jags the blue sky,
whoosh of wind rising
from Ingalls Basin, 1500' below.
From this crest, the craggy south wall
of Mt. Stuart looms across the basin
like a gigantic cutout.
I sit on a serpentinite rock,
catch my breath,
munch on Turkish apricots,
dark chocolate,
and listen.

Do you hear, Tom? The bit
of your ash in this plastic bottle
would be welcome
at the base of the gnarly pine
growing from that narrow rock crevice
on the overhang.

If I steady myself
don't look down
think maybe
I can reach it.

Sorting Things Out

He pockets rolls of quarters left
from his mother's last trip to Las Vegas, lays out

polyester clothes for charity. Here, a notebook
of daily sentences, almost a journal—

place in *keep* pile. A carved stone donkey
from the bedside table, her souvenir letter

opener, *keep both.* Some jewelry he made,
keep, pass on to women friends.

Private messiness of her bureau drawers—
tumble of underwear, old reminder notes,

accumulated film on comb
and brush—*toss*—and pink plastic

hand mirror—*keep, clean later*—confirm
the limits of her orderliness.

He wants to turn his head away,
knows his own tidy kitchen conceals chaos

inside cabinet drawers; his vacuumed bedroom
provides no hint of the wilderness within

the walk-in closet; his well-shaven,
smiling face offers little clue

to a confused heart—
all *kept.*

Humboldt, Tennessee, 1998

with Tommy Dunlop, my father's old friend

His black manservant seats me
in the dark-paneled living room,
brings coffee.

A stooped man in his late 80s
limps in with a cane,
collapses with a grunt into
an overstuffed leather chair,
struggles to focus his long-retired
lawyer's attention,
finally smiles and says
in relaxed West Tennessean:
Good t'meet Lloyd's son.

I thank him and ask a first question
about my long-dead real father.
Tommy settles himself,
begins his narration
lasting over an hour,
leading us back to North Delta farmland
post-WWI, where
the boys chop firewood
to heat their one-room country school,
hike and hunt those round summer mountains
in knee-top boots, and
the business of truck farming.

He tells me my father—youngest of six
surviving siblings—was spoiled,
that he had a car in the '20s. He says:

We'd drive up t'Gibson and Gadsden,
we'd drive out by Fruitland,
stop t'mooch pies and dinners from
relatives.
But mainly we were lookin' for girls..."
He struggles for words—
Man, you shoulda <u>*been*</u> *there!*

I tell him
I'd have liked that
real well.

Message

Small, I'd leap
into the warm mitt
of my father's lap
as he sat in the den's leather chair,
where within his arms
I'd listen to Bible stories, to fairy tales,
then magically wake next morning
in my bed.
After he died at 39
when I was seven,
my mother and uncles decided
I was too young to attend
his funeral.

In my fifties I find him—
buried beyond the Confederate section
of the Humboldt cemetery,
under the shady vase
of an old elm.
He and a brother lie head to head,
share opposite sides
of a 6-foot polished granite block.

I take my time with this meeting,
feel the warm day's first breeze,
place ocean stones on his memorial,
weave soil from my Puget Sound home
into this land of our origin,
glance around the empty grounds,
then lie atop my father.
Close my eyes.

Later, a small insistence
on my left middle finger
calls me from dreamless sleep.
Through my half-opened left eye,
I watch a mockingbird
encode its long tattoo
on my finger.

When We Were Young

...what an enskyment. What a life after death.
—Robinson Jeffers

Spring rains have moistened
this Sonoran Desert where we follow
fragrant fields—lupine, paintbrush,
monkey flowers—into Aravaipa Canyon.
Where winding trail and stream merge,
our low boots
scatter loach minnows and chub.
Midday we shelter under a cottonwood,
watched over by bighorn sheep
patrolling red sandstone cliffs.

We nibble cashews and Jarlsberg,
doze in the shade, then wake
to find vultures circling,
close enough for us to see
their naked red heads.

You laugh. You quote a Jeffers poem.
We vow to return
when we grow old.
We vow to leap
from these high cliffs,
to soar in vulture bellies
our bones picked clean,
left to whiten in the sun.

Back Then

Camping alone,
I fashion a shaving station
atop a streamside log—
same old mirror,
same old razor,
hot water and soap.

Once this act was a threshold
to lying with you in meadows
with bowing avalanche lilies
or in grottoes
of matted beach grass
behind sand dunes,
behind drift logs,
in canyon lands
where we inhaled datura breezes,
sipped spray from red rock waterfalls
high on canyon wren diminuendo,
where we consecrated our nakedness
with war paint from ocher seeps.
Where we hunted each other
through cottonwood bottoms,
through sage land streams,
and into caves
where we wove a snarling love,
a tender love,
then dozed by a starry campfire
watched over by intoxicated bats
and great horned owls.

Back then my face was smooth
as your long-ago breasts.

With Us

Ariel says she feels you
in the early dawn, at the threshold
of sensation. A stirring—not yet head
or elbows. Soon, grandchild,
your contours will speak
and we will know you more.
Yet your presence
is strong in this first wilderness
visit to Yellow Banks—
touchstone in the lives
of your family.

Eagles glide overhead,
hermit crabs and isopods
scurry tide pools, sea otters
play on crusted rocks,
and now—
you.

No Time

Still tasting chocolate bonbon
from the new French bakery
nearby, my three-year-old
grandson suddenly says,
We better hide!
I nod. No time for questions.
He leads us across the busy street
to a hospital courtyard
near the fountain he loves to play in,
then urges us under the dome
of a laceleaf maple,
glances about, and says:
Now we'll be safe.
I point to a necklace
of tiny rocks encircling
the foot of the tree.
Yes, he whispers,
Mama and I made that.
She says it
won't last forever.
Quietly we breathe
till the unnamed danger
passes by.

Fool

He scuttles down
the condo's front steps,

crabs across the brick courtyard, feels
a small face watching over the back

of a couch in an upstairs window.
Head covered by raised shirt,

he spins, flaps arms, contorts
his face, waggles hands in circles.

Giggles from above.
He races through gate

to sidewalk, peers
over wrought iron fence,

judders his neck up and down, waves
the day's goodbye—

ten thousand ways to love
a grandson.

Odyssey

Should we go down, Grampa?
asks five-year-old Tavi.
Worn stairs dissolve in a pool
of gloom, air dank, unbreathed.
Sure, but let's put on our shoes.

With an old cord and hook
I secure the pantry trapdoor and
my keychain squeeze-light
leads us into darkness.

The past whispers
from all directions. A faded
rocking horse grins,
missing one of its marble eyes.
Dusty painting of a dog-man—
round hole for a face—inspires Tavi
to step behind him,
to leer at me
through the opening,
to lend the creature breath, saying
Look at me! Look at me!

We edge our way along narrow pathways
where rusty saws, a hammer, frozen wrenches
beg to be grasped—
Hold me, use me.
Racks of clothes, a crumpled boot
longing for a foot.

Soon there will be no air to breathe,
focus will blur, time will turn to dust.

I think we should leave, Grampa.

Step by step, we creep upward,
step at last into warmth,
where light shards make us blink,
where fresh air swells our chests.

Together we work—
lower the wooden doorway,
replace the boxes that covered it,
hush the mourning below.

On a Tuesday

One-by-one Ms. Wilson's
kindergarteners pop out
through the door she holds open.
Then, behind Awo in her glittering hijab,
ahead of Eiso, his Dutch friend,
Tavi marches out with his purple dinosaur
backpack, eyes seeking mine
among waiting parents.
    Grampa!
    Tavi-man!

Nine blocks to his home,
through a neighborhood
lined with old sycamores, maples,
and mysteries—like this
three-trunked Port Orford cedar,
where he likes to hide,
or these dense shrubs
concealing old bottles
if you know where to look.
Or here—a special rose bush.
He asks me to peel off a thorn,
licks the base and sticks
it to his forehead.
    I'm a rhino!
    Cool, I say.
    Papa showed me how, he says.

Near his second floor condo,
I pull out my key, but his mom,
not at work, opens the door.
    Come in. We have a family emergency.

We follow her upstairs, sit together
on the couch where Tavi likes to bounce.

Papa has left.
He doesn't want to live here anymore.
He's not coming back.
Ever.

Tavi walks into his room,
pulls out his Undersea Legos.
My daughter leans
into my shoulder.
We cry and cry.

After a while I go help Tavi
assemble a deep-sea scuba scooter.

Odonata

As I water container gardens
of kale and lettuce,
snapdragons and geraniums,

a heart-shaped wheel
dances
about my porch.

I dodge the couple,
watch them land
on a nearby gutter.

The male has fitted his tail-tip genitals
to the template on his lady's head, aiding
her own arching tail connection

to his thorax. There, she palpates
his readied sperm packets
into herself.

Such moments must be shared.

I invite my neighbor over.
Once lovers, we stand
on porch chairs to view

large compound eyes, membranous
wings, the sunlit sheen
of diaphanous blues.

Finally the pair disengage,
swirl away through summer greens.
We climb down,

marvel at how life unfolds,
and return
to our separate worlds.

Cornus sericea

Living with your exuberance
near the southwest corner
of my small porch
calls for ongoing negotiation,
definition of boundaries—
a task made difficult by your beauty.
Even now, in late winter, you are irresistible.
Your naked limbs, titian and sensual, hold flocks
of wandering black-capped chickadees
and ruby-crowned kinglets. You must know
I can't resist, though your medusa
ringlets curl my railings,
push away competitors.
As usual, it would be easier if I spoke up
earlier. Eventually I must stand
my ground, reclaim my space.

But for tonight, maybe I'll just
cut one star-flowered stem
to cheer my dinner table.

though never in a Book it lie

At the summit of Navaho Peak,
high on a steep granite ridge,
he realizes: *I'm lonely*.

A gray feather shivers near his boot.
Bone and fur pellets curl nearby.
Was the long-ago counselor right?

You've probably never had a truly intimate relationship.

From a shirt pocket, he fishes Emily D.
To see the Summer Sky / Is Poetry…
Leaning closer, she whispers,

True Poems flee.
They share dried apples, dark chocolate,
peer beyond the snowy crenellations

of the Enchantments.
The warm breeze gentles them
into sleep.

On North 45th Street

The poet,
a Zen priest,
warns us
his 19-foot
accordion-fold poem
has never been read aloud
to an audience
in its entirety.
Forty minutes later
he stops,
asks how we're doing,
then skips ahead.

I leave the bookstore,
not knowing what
to make of this.

Walking to the bus stop
I cross a side lane
where a driver waits to enter
the busy street.
Thinking he sees me,
I step in front.
Then he accelerates.
I leap onto his car hood, screaming.
He brakes.
I land on my feet.
He speeds away.

I have just the strength
of this utility pole
I lean against.
I have just my breath
and this cool night air.

III.

Ripening

Days before I arrive
my mother has the pie aging.
Lemon, butter, condensed milk
soak the graham cracker crust.
She cuts me a wedge—
her lemon pie a disk of sun.

**

To my beaded, bangled girlfriend
I mention Napoleon's famous
request of Josephine—
My dear, avoid bathing three
days prior to my return.
My dear woman adopts the practice.
C'est excellent! Très bien!

**

I thought such tastes
would remain forever.
Not so.
My idea of such pie has long
since replaced
its taste.

Today's breeze off the Strait—
pungent aging kelp
        spiced with basswood blossoms,
served with sunlight.

Old Goat Lake

Hike the Upper Dungeness Trail,
then up a ridge west of Camp Handy.
Steep old fisherman's track
in July afternoon sun.
Thirty steps, gasping stop—thirty more—
old legs and asthmatic lungs
struggling to keep up.
Study huge tree boles,
lush delphiniums before starting again.
Then Goat Lake at last,
air brilliant, snowmelt bubbly.
Bugs not bad. Good night's sleep.
But how much longer
will I be able to rise
after squatting to shit
in these lovely mountains?

Oracles

Clear and cold,
a bubbly tongue of water speaks
of the pass 500 feet higher. The way
rises through melting snow,
through rock grottoes,
basins of avalanche lilies.
Marmot whistles tingle
the thin air.
We climb steep snowdrifts
to grassy ridgetops
southwest of the pass.
We lunch over swapped stories
more truthful
because we are
here.

Nearing 65

Pack lighter than ever,
season late,
I haul myself over headlands
to Toleak Point.
Near this ocean camp,
cow parsnip that
danced in spring breezes
has gone to seed—
leaves slug-nibbled.
Wild lily of the valley,
once a green carpet,
is now yellow and wan.
But listen as north wind rustles
the parsnip's dry pods.
Lower your eyes
to the lily's quiet fruit—
tiny green planets
with maroon continents.

Unburdened

Unbidden, unseen,
the balance of hormones

adjusts as I resist
counteroffers

of blue pills,
testosterone patches.

Lighter than before,
ready for final

ascent, I nonetheless bow
to Eros, who lives

in avalanche lilies, on snowy
ridge crests, and in this rock wall

I am climbing,
hand over hand.

He unravels

dense chords of desire,
hunched at his hearth
on the overcast island
of an inland sea.
He works slowly,
grows old and raw—
listening, thinking,
more conscious of his thirst
when surrounded by water.

Prognosis

He finds himself
at an unmarked junction, shrugs
off his pack to consider.

Coiled on a rocky ledge,
an enormous snake regards him,
tongue flicking.

He asks,
Friend, where
do these paths lead?

To your journey's end,
comes the reply. *Right lies passable trail,*
clear views, though your years might be fewer.

Left, a rough track,
clouded views, though your years
may number more.

The man rubs his head. *Which way*
would you go? Coils ripple. Glistening
eyes meet his.

Shouldering his pack,
he steps carefully over a line
of ants crossing the trail.

When you follow the Big Quil's lead

Big Quilcene River, Olympic Mountains

she tilts time from lowland late summer
to trillium spring, into glacier lily snow melt
and beyond, to cornices of winter. She
dances you through mossy boulder lands
where towers of ancient hemlock and
red cedar groan with wind and time. She lures you
upward with redolence of yellow cedar, cathedrals
of alpine fir, into wildflower heavens of larkspur,
paintbrush and phlox—then delivers you into thin
tundra air where you can share dark chocolate
with God. Beyond Camp Mystery, she reveals her
source, a bubble of icy spring—pure and trustworthy.

She leads you further, recalls times
you followed her to soothe the ache of divorce
or test your failing thyroid on the dizzy and
exhausted trail—where you found
a man 30 years older than you
with new shoulder and heart bypass
also testing himself. And further back to
when she blew your nephews' young minds
by offering a marmot atop a boulder—
surely a mountain wizard,
the shape-shifting benefactor you'd described.
She's called you back from ridges
where you were lost in fog,
grateful for her siren
and the old dog by your side.
She's allowed you to rest
on sunny slopes, reading Dickinson and Han-shan
to her and to your friends.

Recently she pointed to a high perch
where a young Asian couple found you
and your now-barnacled friends
so endearing they took old-guy pictures.

In time she will sigh and offer her way
to your daughter and grandson
heavy with their sack
of ash, up to the pass
where you urinated into Dungeness
and, with a swirl of arching stream,
into Quilcene watersheds. Here, with sweep
of arm, they will cast you on your way
to the Strait of Juan de Fuca, to Puget Sound.

On Cold Mountain

for Han-shan, ca.730 - 850

Centuries dropped away,
distant mountains hazed,
squiggly bonsai trees

our audience.
We sit, study
an ancient go board.

You pause, look up—
How could my poems
have lasted so long?

You tried on my thoughts,
wandered about, made them
your own. Now you sit here,

crazy as me. We shout atari!
into the wind, drink wine,
bum rice cakes

from down at the monastery.
Welcome, brother.
Your move.

Self-Portrait in Plaster

Of all the things this life turned out to be,
an easy trip to the Pure Land was not one.

Might it have helped if my fat belly had been rubbed more,
like my cousins' near doors of Chinese restaurants?

Once I hung out with a short-lived drug queen who admired me,
festooned my upraised arms with beaded necklaces, feather boas.

But I wound up living in this sunporch wilderness
with an arthritic cat, with raccoons making raids on her food.

The old woman who feeds the cat finds common cause
with this decay of my three-foot white plaster body.

When my right arm fell off, she placed it by my side,
then stuck a slim, four-foot branch through my shoulder socket,

down into my hollow body, topped off
by a Christmas ornament—a white-feathered dove.

My *right arm*!
And my butt disassembles in small chunks.

How disappointing this all is—the sunlit porch,
the cedars, the firs, the blue sky.

O Lord! Though I doubt you,
suffuse me with balm,

ladle me Himalayan nectars.
Here I come with crumbling body.

Leap

I always thought there would be white
or maybe blue light
when the time came.
This red surprises.
Fleshy lips
of this precipice
hold the promise
I've yearned for.
Hesitate at the edge,
feel the fire.
No time for timid entry, as
into a mountain lake.
Not this time.

Last Things

High on the Big Quil Trail,
I traverse scree
under Buckhorn’s
basalt pinnacles.
At my feet, the season’s final
scarlet paintbrush.
Where yellow cedars hang,
I climb above the trail,
cut pungent branches
to recall summer days.

A Good Day

At the Tunnel Creek trailhead
an old fellow and his black Labrador
slide from a muddy pickup.
He looks like a logger—
in jeans, suspenders, high boots—
says he's here to admire
fledgling blue grouse.
I hoist my day pack, note the damp weather.
Too bad, he says*, but, really*
every day is a good day.
I say, *No better traveling pal than a black lab.*
Yeah, he says*, it's just me and the dog now.*
My wife died two years ago—
she talked more.

Along this forested stream
all is a shade of green—
huckleberry, wood-fern, vanilla leaf
and towering devil's club,
shiny with recent rain.
Filtered sun angles
through ancient hemlock,
a last bit of warmth
before early frosts.
Where light dapples moss,
two red-spotted garters
slowly twine, prepare
for time below.

Descent

for Tavi

We follow a tangle,
sketchy trails and deer tracks,
then pause in a wilderness
of hemlock and red cedar
where Tavi points to ghostly stalks
reaching up through salal.
I say,
Indian pipe—
some call it corpse plant.
But hey, we better head back to camp.

Sun has slipped low.
Light fades
to a green urgency.

When the trail unravels again
I'm not sure of the way.
Tavi turns to the right.
Think so, man?
He nods.

More sure now, he leads us
through dusk into night.
How can he see?
When the track ends at a drop-off
he leaps from the ledge,
supple as a panther, calls
Come down over this way.

I back down the steep face.
There he takes my hand.

I smile.
He giggles.
And the darkness shimmers.

Photograph by Ariel Meadow Stallings

About the Author

David Stallings was born in the U.S. South, raised in Alaska and Colorado and settled in the Pacific Northwest in the 1970s. Once an academic geographer, he spent many years promoting public transportation in the Puget Sound area. His poems have appeared in North American, U.K. and Swedish literary journals and anthologies, and in *Resurrection Bay* (Evening Street Press).

www.ingramcontent.com/pod-product-compliance
Lightning Source LLC
LaVergne TN
LVHW010107110826
845155LV00028B/525